D1524426

Write It Right

Also by Robert Maidment

Tuning In—A Guide to Effective Listening (1984)
Straight Talk—A Guide to Saying More With Less (1983)
Robert's Rules of Disorder—A Guide to Mismanagement (1976)
Simulation Games—Design and Implementation (1973)
Criticism, Conflict, and Change (1970)

Write It Right

A Guide To
Better Messages

ROBERT MAIDMENT

PELICAN PUBLISHING COMPANY

GRETNA 1987

Library of Congress Cataloging-in-Publication Data

Maidment, Robert.
    Write it right.

    1. Rhetoric. I. Title.
PN163.M35   1987   808'.042   87-2247
ISBN: 0-88289-647-4

Manufactured in the United States of America
Published by Pelican Publishing Company, Inc.
1101 Monroe Street, Gretna, Louisiana 70053

This book is dedicated to
physician and publisher Milburn Calhoun
who keeps his writers healthy
in two *ways.*

Contents

Preface

Words. To be read someone must write them. As the Bard might note, "therein lies the rub." But the rub for non-authors is an eraser. While professional writers work while writing, the rest of us write while working. Pros and amateurs do agree that writing inch-by-inch is no cinch. As John Updike observes, "Writing and rewriting is a constant search for what it is one is saying."

Now that more printed information and electronically transmitted data need to be exchanged, more care must be exercised in assuring accuracy, brevity, and clarity. It is a personal victory and no small miracle each time we know for certain that some similarity exists between the message we intend to send and the one understood by our reader.

The assorted notations in this volume can assist non-writers in preparing memoranda, letters, and reports. This is *not* a technical manual. A reader will sense a mild disdain for the "purveyors of preciseness" in writing. We're advocating effective, not perfect messages. As Thoreau wryly noted, "Any fool can make a rule and every fool will mind it."

If you're willing to apply the suggestions that follow, your written messages will be shorter and sharper. Guaranteed! A point-counterpoint format is used. The counterpoint adds a related, contrasting, heretical, or diversionary note.

We write alone, receive little support, and even less appreciation. Since writing is playing with one's mental blocks, we might as well enjoy the process in our quest to write it right.

Acknowledgments

Someone else *always* writes it better. Proof rests with the words of J. Scott Armstrong, C. E. Ayres, Maggie Barnes, The Red Baron, Robert Bernstein, Ambrose Bierce, Thomas C. Blaisdell, Joy Blake, Lawrence Block, Lynn Z. Bloom, Dave Blum, Napoleon Bonaparte, Philip Broughton, Albert Camus, e. e. cummings, Salvador Dali, John Dewey, Joan Didion, Peter F. Drucker, T. S. Eliot, E. M. Forster, Kahlil Gibran, Martin L. Gibson, Jim Grant, Gilbert Grosvenor, Robert Gunning, S. I. Hayakawa, Robert Heinlein, Ernest Hemingway, Takashi Ishihara, Anthony Jay, Samuel Johnson, Franklin P. Jones, Charlton Laird, Walter S. Landor, John Lehman, David Lilienthal, Vince Lombardi, Ron McDole, Dwight Macdonald, John D. MacDonald, Marianne Moore, Wilson Mizner, Grandma Moses, Moses, John Naisbitt, Pascal, Joseph C. Pattison, George S. Patton, Lawrence J. Peter, Jean Piaget, Plato, Popeye, Fred Pryor, Don Ried, William Safire, Susan Polis Schutz, William Shakespeare, George Bernard Shaw, Red Smith, Sydney Smith, Gertrude Stein, William Strunk, Ross Thomas, Henry David Thoreau, Anne Davis Toppins, James Thurber, Mark Twain, John Updike, United Technologies Corporation, Hugh Walpole, E. B. White, Winnie the Pooh, Woodrow Wilson, Herman Wouk, J. M. Ziman, William Zinsser, and the Harvard Committee on Composition and Rhetoric. Thank you.

Say it
Stop it
Scan it
Sign it
Stuff it
Seal it
Stamp it
Send it

—Straight Talk

Write It Right

Despair Not

POINT

While some of us have an occasional itch to scribble, we suspect that we'd rather switch than scratch. We certainly prepared ourselves to write. In twelve years of house arrest in a place called school we devoted more time to writing skills than to recess. If we did so much of it, then why aren't we more proficient? Well, dull and dreary drill spawned that widespread malady, "painmanship," with those familiar it-hurts-to-write symptoms. Despair not. The following pages provide a partial, but painless, cure for those times when we *have* to write.

COUNTERPOINT

The ninety and nine will write letters throughout life, and they will write nothing else.

—Thomas C. Blaisdell

19

Fear No Error

POINT

When we speak we edit in process by correcting and clarifying. Not so when we write. We jot and send, or edit and print. And once sent it sticks. Permanent ink. If our musings were engraved on self-destruct paper, they would vaporize after a few readings. While errant phrases and predictions haunt us, fearing sins of the pen hurts us more. We can't always write it right, but we can improve the odds.

COUNTERPOINT

As long as we insist upon writing with errors, at least we can invent some *new* ones.

Gain Initial Interest

POINT

Do the initial words of your letters "open doors"? Sales personnel know that the first moments with a customer can mean the difference between a foot in the door and a door in the face. Our letters serve as door openers for creating new relationships, continuing old ones, or cementing broken ones. Opening lines such as "I know you don't want to be reminded of . . . ," "It has come to my attention that . . . ," "I regret to inform you that . . . ," or "If you will recall our conversation last month . . . ," are unlikely to arouse reader interest. Beginning words make lingering impressions.

COUNTERPOINT

Please excuse such a long letter; I don't have time to write a short one.

—Pascal

Put It Down Without Putting It Down

POINT

Admittedly, writing isn't one of our favorite work or leisure pursuits. Even though learning to write consumed more hours of our schooling than anything else, business leaders invest less than ten percent of their workday in various writing activities. We can sympathize with the wag who lamented, "Whenever I feel like writing, I lie down until the feeling goes away." Some of our avoidance can be explained since for most of us writing, unlike talking or reading, is *work*. And we need not apologize for that—at least not while the meter's running. Besides, we can't nap on the job.

COUNTERPOINT

Writing is not necessarily something to be ashamed of—but do it in private and wash your hands afterward.

—Robert Heinlein

Talk with a Pen

POINT

You can't tell a prefix from a suffix? Don't know a synonym for antonym? Confused by homophones? Here's some refreshing news—you can *forget* them! Although we agree with critic Dwight Macdonald's warning that "Simple illiteracy is no basis for linguistic evolution," one needn't be a grammarian to write. If you can think it, you can say it, and you can write what you say. Now others can read what you write.

COUNTERPOINT

It is a little less than absurd to suggest that any human who can be taught to talk cannot likewise be taught to compose. Writing is merely the habit of talking with the pen instead of the tongue.

—Harvard Committee on
Composition and Rhetoric (1902)

Maintain a Positive Tone

POINT

A vast array of books urges us to examine ourselves in a positive manner, to expect the best from one another, and to extract the maximum benefit from every golden moment. Just as we are so is our writing. Our words on paper display our thoughts and convey them in subtle ways with a tone of their own. Our words reflect basic attitudes ranging from gloom to gleam. Negative thinking breeds negative writing. And negative writing infects the breeder *and* the reader.

COUNTERPOINT

We're loaded down with yesterday—any organism has to be able to get rid of its waste products or it will drown in its own toxic waste.

—PETER F. DRUCKER

Squeeze It

POINT

Why write "at the present time" or "in the very near future" when "now" and "soon" say it with seven fewer words? A most common unnecessarily expanded expression is "in view of the fact that" when a simple "because" or "since" suffices. Squeeze these: "at a later date," "for the purpose of," "will you be kind enough to," "in this day and age," and "along the lines of." Did you think "later," "for," "please," "today," and "like"? Congratulations. You just ditched eighteen words and fifty-five letters!

COUNTERPOINT

> The written word
> Should be clean as bone!
> Clear as light
> Firm as stone;
> Two words are not
> As good as one.

> —ANON

The Fog Index

(150-word letter with 10 sentences and
15 "hard" words)

Average sentence length (150 ÷ 10)	15
Percent of hard words (15 ÷ 150)	+ 10%
	25
Fog Index Factor	× .4
Fog Index	10

—ROBERT GUNNING

Check the Fog

POINT

Robert Gunning designed a "fog index" to determine the readability of our writing. His index yields the level of schooling needed to read material with ease—an index over 12 causes some difficulty for most. To determine the reading difficulty of your writing: (1) Isolate a 200-word sample, (2) Find the average sentence length by dividing the number of words by the number of sentences, (3) Count the number of words with 3 or more syllables, eliminating proper nouns and "ed" or "es" words, (4) Divide #3 by the total words in your sample, (5) Despite the questionable arithmetic, add #2 and #4, and (6) Multiply by the fog index factor, .4 (see example at left). Try it. You might be surprised.

COUNTERPOINT

We can write:
"A maleficent horizontally
propelled current of gaseous
matter is not the harbinger
of a modicum of beneficence"
        or
"An ill wind blows no good."
The choice is ours.

Shorten with Caution

POINT

William Strunk and E. B. White in their classic book, *The Elements of Style,* write, "A sentence should contain no unnecessary words, a paragraph no unnecessary sentences, for the same reason that a drawing should have no unnecessary lines and a machine no unnecessary parts." With apologies to Strunk & White we could rewrite *their* sentence: "Sentences and paragraphs, not unlike drawings and machines, don't need extra words, lines, or parts." Thirty words were reduced to fifteen. Is our sentence twice as good because half of the so-called unnecessary words were eliminated? No, Strunk & White make their point with style. Fewer is not always better.

COUNTERPOINT

> Overstate and bore.
> Understate and score.
> When a baseball umpire says,
> "Strike three!"
> He doesn't have to add
> "Yer out."
> That's what strike three means.

—AD MESSAGE
United Technologies Corporation

Plan It First

POINT

Humorist James Thurber once admonished, "I don't believe the writer should know too much where he's going. If he does, he runs into old man blueprint—old man propaganda." Overplanning, of course, can yield stilted prose. The problem is knowing precisely when we've planned far ahead enough. Knowing up front *what* we're about to write—information from gathered thoughts, notes, or outlines—does enable more attention to be focused upon *how* we're going to write it. Careful planning is the key ingredient of improvisation.

COUNTERPOINT

Nothing beats good planning more than dumb luck.

Reduce the Redundancies

POINT

One baffling enigma we want to make perfectly clear is the true facts concerning redundancies. Of course, we don't need the words "baffling," "perfectly," or "true." Why do we insist upon saying so many things twice? We're invited to an "advance planning session," warned of a "serious crisis," touted on a "new innovation," told that something is "very unique," strive for "a consensus of opinion," and schedule a trip during the "month of February." For once and for all can't we utterly reject all such phrases that are visible to the eye or tangible enough to be felt?

COUNTERPOINT

Three things we Germans are famous for:

Promptness,
Punctuality, and
Not being late.

—THE RED BARON
Lufthansa Advertisement

Attend to Reader Needs

POINT

Once I've written a directive, I think, "Have I included everything? Will my readers still have questions?" It's time to apply the Who, What, Why, Where, When, How Answers Test (WWWWWHAT). Attending to these "5W's and 1 H" virtually assures completeness. I can assume I've included everything. Now, if readers still have questions, it's *their* problem! WWWWWHAT?

COUNTERPOINT

The difficulty with written communication is the assumption that we have accomplished it.

Write to Influence

POINT

Lists of leadership traits often include a reference to facility with "persuasive written communication." One initially ascends the leader ladder via drift, draft, design, or divine intervention. How *high* the climb in most corporate settings, however, is often linked to one's ability to write succinctly and persuasively. Those who conduct seminars and workshops especially designed to enhance business writing skills consistently stress techniques of persuasive writing. How we've learned to write is apparently unrelated to what we need to know about writing.

COUNTERPOINT

The subject of management is man; the objective of management is the moving of man's mind and will and imagination.

—David E. Lilienthal

Avoid Subjectivity

POINT

The following sentences are likely to arouse a reader in different ways:

- We've got a sloppy billing system.
- Within the past week 5 customers were billed for unordered merchandise while 3 others received no credit for returned goods.

Obviously, the second sentence is more specific and the *reader* thinks, "We've got a sloppy operation that needs immediate attention." The first sentence, judgmentally loaded, is more likely to incite than to inspire.

COUNTERPOINT

The discipline of keeping the subjective mind under control is, even though imperfect, vastly exhausting.

—JOHN D. MACDONALD
No Deadly Drug

Be Brief

POINT

The escalating pace of change requires us to read more to remain reasonably current. If we were mindful of the myriad demands placed upon our reader, we'd not ramble endlessly. Say it and stop. Short, punchy letters and reports are read sooner, faster, and more often. More importantly, crisper messages are remembered longer and more accurately by the reader. Need we write more?

COUNTERPOINT

I shall be so brief that I have already finished.

—SALVADOR DALI

Be Briefer

POINT

A classic story about brevity cites a fishmonger seeking to replace the weathered sign over his market stall: FRESH FISH SOLD HERE DAILY. Shocked by an estimate in which a single letter would cost more than the entire original, the fishmonger negotiated with the signpainter. Wanting the job, the signpainter suggested, "Look, you're open seven days so DAILY goes. You've been at this location for 30 years so HERE goes too. And you obviously *sell* fish so SOLD goes as well." Inhaling deeply, the signpainter reckoned that even FRESH could be misleading. The fishmonger happily agreed to a new, low-budget sign: FISH!

COUNTERPOINT

Writing with brevity is like the relationship between a fan and the fan dancer—attention is invited to the subject but no effort is made to cover it entirely.

WRITE IT RIGHT NO. 17
Be Briefer Still

POINT

On average we listen to the equivalent of a book per day, a talk sufficiently to fill a book a week, read a book a month, and write enough to fill a book a year. Let's focus upon the last "book." We can lessen the print glut by writing only when we have sound reason to do so. Can you imagine how much writing, reading, sending, sorting, and copying or shredding time could be saved if everyone in every organization ignored the motive to write and awaited a sound reason? Be briefer still and don't write at all.

COUNTERPOINT

One needs a motive, if not a sound reason, to go to Los Angeles, just as one needs a motive, but not necessarily a sound reason, to commit murder. This is probably because motives don't require good sense, while sound reasons almost always do.

—Ross Thomas
The Money Harvest

Use the Right Tools

POINT

Beyond pen and paper we need an appropriate mix of minimal literacy, motivation, and material to write about. (Yes, a preposition is a bad thing to end a sentence with.) Still impossible, you say, to write with some precision? Three reference books can resolve ninety-eight percent of whatever writing dilemmas remain: (1) a current unabridged dictionary for spellings, new words, definitions, and updated usage; (2) a thesaurus, the "dictionary-within-a-dictionary," for quickly locating alternative words and subtle meanings; and (3) a high school grammar text for traditional usage. The other two percent? Only a language purist will detect your errors. If what you write is to be published, however, dare an editor to find them!

COUNTERPOINT

Impossibility: a word only to be found in the dictionary of fools.

—NAPOLEON BONAPARTE

Learn by Reading

POINT

As philosopher John Dewey frequently implored, "We learn by doing." To enhance any skill, you must use it, so obviously nothing improves writing more than writing itself. There is also a useful relationship between reading and writing. Although we can't master windsurfing from a book, we can learn more about writing by reading. We can note how the style and rhythm of a writer's words convey charm, clarity, logic, influence, creativity, credibility, humor, power, and other important features. Of course, if a writer is effective, perhaps we'll be unaware of anything other than the ideas expressed.

COUNTERPOINT

I never desire to converse with a man who has written more than he has read.

—SAMUEL JOHNSON

Go with What You've Got

POINT

Before writing a letter or report we normally go through a "get smart" stage of fact gathering and idea generating. The problem, naturally, is that all of the information we need isn't at hand. Options include waiting for the missing material, writing without it, or "winging it" with contrived data. These actions inexorably yield missed deadlines, inexactness, or loss of credibility. Since having *all* of the needed information is rare, perhaps we should go with what we have, honestly, and on time.

COUNTERPOINT

The information we have is not what we want, the information we want is not what we need, and the information we need is not available.

—FINAGLE'S LAW

Start at Ground Level

POINT

According to writer William Zinsser, "The most important sentence in any article is the first one. If it doesn't induce the reader to proceed to the second sentence, your article is dead." In all business writing we must provide initial, vital baseline data because our reader is likely to ask: (1) What is this about? (2) Why is this of importance to me? and (3) Do I need to read further? When we don't start our readers at ground level before launching them skyward, they'll divert their attention elsewhere.

COUNTERPOINT

Interviewer: "How do you paint?"

Grandma Moses: "Down. I paint the sky, then the trees, then the land."

Curtail Acronyms

POINT

Military writers can string together a dazzling array of initials (CINCLANT) and acronyms (NORAD) that their readers can apparently decipher. A steady diet of alphabet soup, however, is discomforting. Translating acronyms when first used is a small, but welcome concession for those who forgot or never knew. Does RIF, for example, mean Reduction in Force or Reading is Fun? If you're a victim of the former, perhaps you have time to benefit from the latter.

COUNTERPOINT

If you think OSHA is a Wisconsin city you're in trouble.

Stash the Slang

POINT

Many of us recall when one mowed grass and stewed in a pot. Admittedly, it is hard to keep pace with a rapidly expanding lexicon. If we are among the first to circulate newly minted verbal currency in writing, we invite confusion. Remember when you first heard "bad" used to mean "good"? While the "in" crowd understands, the "out" crowd remains out. One solution is to "cop some z's" until the outs are in.

COUNTERPOINT

IF IN DOUBT, PUNK

PUNK (Circa 1945)	Heat	(Lighting fireworks)
PUNK (Circa 1955)	Health	(Feeling lousy)
PUNK (Circa 1965)	Hoodlum	(Acting bad)
PUNK (Circa 1985)	Hard rock	(Performing music)

Ban All Abbrs.

POINT

We propose a quick, quiet interment for most abbreviations. Latin ones are particularly troublesome:

e.g. exempli gratia (for example)
i.e. id est (that is)
etc. et cetera (and so forth)

We often write i.e. when we mean e.g., and, besides, correctly punctuating them is difficult. Especially irritating is "etc.," as in red, orange, yellow, etc. Did the writer forget the rest of the spectrum? Is the reader free to add taupe, fuchsia, and heliotrope? Why not write red, orange, yellow, and assorted colors? Or simply red, orange, and (*not* "&") yellow?

COUNTERPOINT

When in doubt, write it out.

—JOY BLAKE

Stay in Command

POINT

In *Caine Mutiny* Herman Wouk's memorable Captain Queeg cites four ways to execute a task: "The right way, the wrong way, the Navy way, and *my* way." Writing entrepreneurially, or "my way," spells t-r-o-u-b-l-e. While poet e. e. cummings could flout upper case letters and flourish, we can't. The safest course, of course, is the "right way." When we lose our command of English we, like Queeg, lose our command.

COUNTERPOINT

It's not wise to violate rules until you know how to use them.

—T. S. ELIOT

Write What You Mean

POINT

Tentativeness erodes credibility: I'm not certain, but . . . ; It seems as if . . . ; or We will probably. . . . Whatever follows will (1) cause the reader to doubt your message and, of more consequence, (2) cause the reader to doubt *you*. We can take a lesson from Popeye: "I say what I mean and mean what I say!" Perhaps if we can't, we shouldn't.

COUNTERPOINT

I've got a sort of idea but I don't suppose it's a very good one.

—WINNIE THE POOH

Say It and Stop

POINT

We implore public speakers to tell us what they intend to say, to tell us, and, finally, to tell us what we've been told. This ritual works for speakers since a listener can't hear twice what is said once. Readers, however, can skim or scan at will. The message for writers is quite clear—say it once and stop. Don't gamble with a ramble.

COUNTERPOINT

While eyes may be windows to the soul, the mouth is not necessarily a door to the brain.

Remove Self-Imposed Barriers

POINT

On-the-job writing is a task quite unlike off-duty creative expression and personal jottings. Various work-related barriers such as a mandated writing style or unrealistic deadlines come with the territory. Blaming these impediments to writing, however, is a cop-out. Conversely, other restraints such as a perceived lack of skill or a lack of interest in the writing assignment are self-imposed. Hiding behind these barriers becomes an exercise in self-deception.

COUNTERPOINT

We will be better and braver if we engage and inquire than if we indulge in the idle fancy that we already know or that it is of no use to know what we do not.

—PLATO

Use Persuasive Words

POINT

Car dealer to potential buyer: "A smart buyer like you would make a down payment today." While we hear "smart buyer" and silently discount the salesman's pitch, we miss the implanted command, "make a down payment today." Purportedly, the twelve most powerful words are: results, proven, guarantee, save, money, you, new, health, easy, safety, love, and discovery. Scattering these words throughout our letters probably won't persuade any reader to do anything. Expressing clearly whatever *benefit* will positively affect the reader, however, is powerfully persuasive.

COUNTERPOINT

The ten most persuasive advertising words: new, save, free, natural, rich, real, fresh, extra, discover, and light.

Suggestion for a beer commercial: *Discover* the *rich* taste of our *new natural light*. *Save* on price and get *real fresh* flavor, *free* of *extra* calories.

Write It Now

POINT

We are tempted to delay rather than tackle unpleasant tasks. What can we do when a writing assignment falls to us? Simple. Do it *now.* If time management is really self-management, and if the flip side of time management is stress management, the more we delay the more stressful the task. Some claim that as pressure increases so does productivity. Perhaps. But what happens to quality?

COUNTERPOINT

A good plan violently executed right now is far better than a perfect plan executed next week.

—GENERAL GEORGE S. PATTON

Proof It Once

POINT

If only our writing would magically fade once read. Errors in writing, that is—we want the good stuff to last. Recall the sales rep who sent a mailgram to a major customer reading, "We are not prepared to ship the 10,000 widgets you ordered." He intended to write "now," not "not." Only one little letter in only one little three-letter word. This message outlasted the unsold widgets. Even today in sales training sessions someone predictably comments upon the episode: "Once we had this sales rep who. . . ." Proof it or goof it.

COUNTERPOINT

Those who write clearly have readers; those who write obscurely have commentators.

—ALBERT CAMUS

Proof It Twice

POINT

Occasionally, we write a correct message but convey an unintended meaning. For example, you need thirty photocopies of a report for a staff meeting. The material is delivered with a cover note from the office manager: "Here are the 30 copies you requested." An innocuous note? Not if you mentally underscore "30" and assume the writer is on another economy kick. Dropping the number or adding a second sentence, "Please let me know if you need more," is more comforting—that wasn't such an extravagant request after all! Although it is impossible to predict what others will read into our messages, we can reduce the possibility of distortion by proofing a second time and asking, "What *other* possible meanings could this message have?"

COUNTERPOINT

The memory is a cooperative animal, eager to please; what it cannot supply it occasionally invents, sketching carefully to fill in the blanks.

—LAWRENCE BLOCK
A Stab in the Dark

Proof It Once More

POINT

Purposeful communication is an effort to achieve similar meaning between sender and receiver. The key word is "similar" since we rarely achieve *identical* meanings in written communication. Certainly, a few messages, like "Thou shalt not kill," leave little doubt. Unlike Moses, however, we're unlikely to leave ten such consecutive sentences as part of our legacy in a lifetime of writing. So content ourselves we must with "similar." Our heavenly lament: Give us the whole proof and nothing but the proof—so help us plod!

COUNTERPOINT

Mark everything that strikes you. I may consider a thing 49 times; but if you consider it, it will be considered 50 times; and a line 50 times considered is 2 per cent better than a line 49 times considered. And it is the final 2 per cent that makes the difference between excellence and mediocrity.

—George Bernard Shaw
(to a reviewer of his manuscripts)

Recite, Then Rewrite

POINT

Admittedly, successful proofing requires us to see the errors. If a rereading suggests "that-doesn't-*look*-right," recite the offending sentence for the "that-doesn't-sound-right" effect. Flunk the "test"? You're probably right; what you wrote was wrong. Example: Everyone (will, shall) have (his, her, their, his or her) opportunity to report (his, her) progress at our next meeting. However written, it's not likely to look or sound correct. Try the "I won't use it at all" approach and write: Be prepared to give a progress report at our next meeting. Strike back, not out.

COUNTERPOINT

How do I know what I think until I see what I say?

—E. M. FORSTER

Choose the Right Word

POINT

Choosing (selecting, picking out) the right (correct, appropriate) words when we write is hard (difficult, arduous). The 2,000 words we use most have over 20,000 meanings. The word "cut," for example, can mean lop, saw, nip, hew, mow, or bob—and these are only three-letter varieties of "cut." We can be concise without always being precise. In the first sentence above why use "picking out" when one word will do? Or why use the four-syllable "appropriate" when "right" does the job? And since "arduous" suggests strenuous *physical* effort, why use it?

COUNTERPOINT

The difference between the right word and the almost right word is the difference between lightning and a lightning bug.

—MARK TWAIN

Be Artfully Crafty

POINT

A few words about writing subtleties, those mental morsels that spice our prose providing food for ideation or indigestion. While subtleties display one's mental agility, the line separating keen from crafty or acuteness from cunning is very thin. The problem, of course, is that we're unnecessarily burdening our readers. Only when we're reasonably assured that our reader can make the intended connections is it safe to be subtle.

COUNTERPOINT

Fly over everybody's head only when your purpose is to teach or to tease.

—WILLIAM SAFIRE

Banish Sexism

POINT

Attempts to banish sexism in language have spawned neutered words (chairperson) and revised job descriptions (flight attendant). Along with these overdue changes we've also created an incredibly clumsy hybrid—"his and her" (or, worse, "his/her") to displace the ubiquitous and biased "his." Instead of writing "Every employee should complete his or her whatever," we can use the inclusive *their* as in "All employees should complete their whatever." Words like "staff" or "personnel" are also cleaner, simpler, all-inclusive, and—asexual.

COUNTERPOINT

THE OBJECTIVE INTERVIEW

"Can you type?"
"No!"
"Can you file?"
"No!"
"Can you take shorthand?"
"No!"
"How about simple bookkeeping?"
"No!"
"What on earth can you do?"
"Everything you can!"

—SUSAN POLIS SCHUTZ

Use the Active Voice

POINT

Rather than cite reasons for writing in the active voice, we'll focus on a defect in the passive. How do you respond to these examples:

- The materials were ordered and were found to be unsatisfactory. (passive)
- I am dissatisfied with my order. (active)

  The first writer shirks responsibility for (1) ordering the materials and (2) rating them unsatisfactory. Predictably, in corporate settings managers frequently use the passive voice, because who eagerly claims ownership for anything that doesn't work? The notion that the first example is more "polite" doesn't wash. If you have a choice, use the active voice.

COUNTERPOINT

Five Stages of a Corporate Action

1. Wild enthusiasm
2. Disillusionment
3. Search for the guilty
4. Conviction of the innocent
5. Promotion of the uninvolved

—SOURCE UNKNOWN

Immediately Record Critical Data

POINT

There are a few situations when the timing of our writing is critical. Documenting sensitive material prior to a dismissal hearing is one such occasion. When we must record such observations is clear. *Now!* To delay is to distort. Any file of critical incidents should reflect accurately what the observer saw as soon after the fact as possible. Both time and trials often thrive upon subsequently embellished data at our expense.

COUNTERPOINT

It didn't happen if you didn't see it, and you didn't see it if you didn't write it down.

Expunge the X-Rated

POINT

When novelists pen the profane, they portray a slice of life. An even slightly salty business letter, however, can become the spice of strife. Any X-rated material is predictably noted with varying degrees of acceptance and, unfortunately, is fixed in memory. A negative reaction can adversely affect a future exchange between reader and writer. So be profound, not profane. Risqué writing is risky.

COUNTERPOINT

It's usually OK to call a spade a spade.
It's never OK to call it a ****** shovel.

Drain the Clogs

POINT

Shorter, unfamiliar words can also overload reader circuitry. If you intend to annoy a respondent, try using "turgid," "torpid," or "turbid" in your next message. Now these are particularly useful words if you're seeking six-letter crossword solutions for "swollen," "sluggish," or "stirred-up." If not, you're probably clogging someone else's brain.

COUNTERPOINT

> Clear writers, like fountains,
> Do not seem so deep as they are;
> The turbid look the most profound.

—Walter S. Landor

Add Some Strokes

POINT

Once your word processor rapid-prints neat, clean, and impersonal copies of an in-house directive or memo, would you defile it other than by perfunctory initialing? Most managers wouldn't. Some companies *encourage* adding highlighted markings and handwritten notes to internal messages. There are two advantages. First, the reader zeros-in on critical data and crucial deadlines. And even more importantly, the added notes and strokes suggest that the message is especially written for a special reader.

COUNTERPOINT

The more high technology around us, the more the need for human touch.

—JOHN NAISBITT
Megatrends

WRITE IT RIGHT NO. 43
Acknowledge Errors

POINT

We write, revise, proof, and invite collegial review. Everything is fine because surviving errors only surface when we distribute. Then very shortly someone, somewhere, will detect the slightest flaw. What to do? Thank the sleuth publicly and admit privately that your fail-safe effort wasn't. If the error is substantial, declare responsibility and take remedial action. If minuscule, add it to your list of mistakes to avoid next time. And if you can, delete the sleuth from future mailings. Just kidding, of course.

COUNTERPOINT

Noted in a newsletter:

> Someone said there were a number of typos in the last issue. Purely an unsubstantiated rumor. Our regular readers know we never make mistrakes.

—MAGGIE BARNES

Test the Logic

POINT

While viewing a television commercial claiming that an antacid could absorb thirty-nine times its weight in concentrated stomach acid, I could imagine being totally consumed by a single, five-pound tablet. And that's *not* how to spell relief! We're media-blitzed daily with absurd or spurious commentary. An embarrassing oversight in writing is to confuse correlation with causation. Events can occur in concert or sequence by chance or by design. Failing to note the difference can erode our credibility. Test fly before you testify.

COUNTERPOINT

Roger's Law: As soon as the flight attendant serves coffee, the airliner encounters turbulence.

Davis' Explanation of Roger's Law: Serving coffee on aircraft causes turbulence.

WRITE IT RIGHT NO. 45
Purge the Jargon

POINT

Several new words—"bureaucratese," "gobbledygook," "edubabble," "bafflegab"—have been coined to describe any multisyllabic jargon designed to obfuscate and destined for obscurity. Such fuzzy phrasing is often linked to federal agencies generally and to the helping professions specifically. Philip Broughton created a buzzword generator (below) to assist those with a penchant for pompous writing. One simply selects any three-digit number from his three-column list (6-4-3, for example, yields "optional digital capability"). Plaudits to Philip for purging the purveyors of pretentious, portentous prose!

COUNTERPOINT

Systematic Buzz Phrase Projector

	A	B	C
0)	integrated	management	options
1)	total	organizational	flexibility
2)	systematized	monitored	capability
3)	parallel	reciprocal	mobility
4)	functional	digital	programming
5)	responsive	logistical	concept
6)	optional	transitional	time-phase
7)	synchronized	incremental	projection
8)	compatible	third-generation	hardware
9)	balanced	policy	contingency

—PHILIP BROUGHTON

Add Some "Pictures"

POINT

Appropriate graphics can improve reader recall. The chart below indicates recall rates with and without graphics for periods of three hours and three days. The sixty-five percent, three-day recall percentage is impressive. We can only "prove" our point by asking: Is the chart helpful?

COUNTERPOINT

The writer's goal is to communicate with the largest possible number of readers. . . . You have a series of pictures in your head which you reduce to words on paper. . . . Your goal is to make the pictures in your readers' heads resemble the pictures in your head. If you agree on certain things—the meanings of most words, for instance—the process will work.

—MARTIN L. GIBSON
Editing in the Electronic Era

METHOD OF PRESENTATION	RECALL 3 HOURS LATER	RECALL 3 DAYS LATER
WORDS ONLY	70%	10%
GRAPHICS ONLY	72%	20%
WORDS SUPPORTED BY GRAPHICS	85%	65%

Strive for Perfection

POINT

What does a *perfect* letter look like? I've carefully preserved my nomination for the clearest and briefest specimen. A colleague was nearing completion of a public television studio when some miscreants absconded with his sophisticated, expensive, and underinsured equipment. Sandwiched between the Dear Bob and Sincerely was his anger and frustration vented in one onomatopoetic primal scream: AAAAAAARRRRRGGGH! Perfect letter(s) indeed.

COUNTERPOINT

Language is the system of various noises humans produce with their lungs, throats, tongues, teeth, and lips systematically standing for specified happenings in their nervous system.

—S. I. HAYAKAWA
Language in Thought and Action

Risk a Collegial Review

POINT

Ask a colleague to review your correspondence. Retain a copy file of nonconfidential, nonroutine letters and memos. Now share them periodically with an associate who is willing to review and to reciprocate. Your colleague will note an occasional misstatement, redundancy, or obfuscation. Any unintentional breach in cordiality or emotional tone will also be noticed. Not only will each of you enhance your editing skills, but you will also be alerted to things you missed in the originals.

COUNTERPOINT

> I'm not trying to set any records,
> I'm just trying to keep you alert.

—CROSS-EYED JAVELIN THROWER

Let Your Errors Be Original Ones

POINT

We promised no grammar lessons. Would you accept a slight exception? During two decades of affixing red marks upon graduate student themes I've kept an informal frequency count of common writing errors. Here are a few of the "winners":

- most frequent misspelling — accommodate (it has 2 c's *and* 2 m's)
- most frequent word misuse — affect and effect (only a dictionary can resolve this one)
- most frequent punctuation error — omitting the possessive (Murphy's Law not Murphys Law)
- most frequent subject-verb disagreement — criterion followed by a plural verb (The major criterion for evaluating personnel is (*not* are)_ _ _ .)
- most frequent use of a non-existent word — irregardless (with "prioritize" a close second)

Have I included any of your favorite errors?

COUNTERPOINT

The Handy-Dandy Grammar Guide

- Don't use no double negatives.
- Make each pronoun agree with their antecedent.
- Join clauses good, like a conjunction should.
- About them sentence fragments.
- When dangling, watch your participles.
- Verbs has to agree with their subjects.
- Just between you and I, case is important too.
- Don't write run-on sentences they are hard to read.
- Don't use commas, which aren't necessary.
- Try to not ever split infinitives.
- Its important to use your apostrophe's correctly.
- Proofread your writing to see if you any words out.
- Correct spelling is esential.

—AUTHOR UNKNOWN OR
INTENTIONALLY ANONYMOUS

WRITE IT RIGHT NO. 50
Communicate Confidence

POINT

It is important to convey the appropriate level of confidence in our business writing. But even a slight stretching of confidence conveys arrogance. When we indulge in boastful commentary, we predictably erode our credibility. Only when we transmit reasonable expectations for person or product do we automatically transfer a measure of confidence. The "what-you-see-is-what-you-get" approach works only when what you want is deliverable.

COUNTERPOINT

We didn't lose any games last season, we just ran out of time twice.

—Vince Lombardi

Post Haste

POINT

I'm a speed letter freak. Speed letters are those easy-mailing, telegram-size, urgent-looking, single- or multi-carbon, lined blanks for sending messages. The reader typically reacts by adding a note, signing, and remailing. Speed letters are seldom shuffled to a pile of unanswered correspondence, require no secretarial assistance, provide an instant copy, and virtually guarantee a prompt reply. Best of all both initiator and respondent are limited by space to shortness of breadth.

COUNTERPOINT

The writer does the most who gives his reader the most knowledge, and takes from him the least time.

—SYDNEY SMITH

Write Domestic

POINT

Why do some people insist upon using "foreign" expressions? To impress? Whenever I read the French *vis-à-vis*, I must stop and translate. Did the writer mean "compared with," "face-to-face," or "opposite to"? And when encountering the Latin *quid pro quo*, I must decide if the writer intended "substitute for" or "something equivalent." Roman numerals above ten are also deadly. While both LXXX and XXC are correct, 80 is easier. Translate for those of us who aren't polylingual. Better yet, write domestic.

COUNTERPOINT

We should write to express and not to impress.
N'est-ce pas? (Isn't that so?)

Write Out Your Emotions

POINT

When encountering situations that cause our emotional temperature to escalate, we scream, sulk, swear, or slam doors in response. One colleague was prone to pitch a rubber brick until a ricochet smashed his desk lamp. Writing can be a therapeutic method for quiet venting while conveying to others that you are productively occupied. Write a letter to the offender. Dispense with the pleasantries and let the passion flow. Now shred it and forget it. Subsequent poisonless pen letters will be better, not bitter.

COUNTERPOINT

How did "sugar, spice, and everything nice" ever become "acid, lemon, and filled with venom"?

Censor All Clichés

POINT

A cliché is an expression worn thin through chronic abuse. As they say, "familiarity breeds contempt." Don't you "love to hate" such gems as "playing with a full deck," "getting more bang for the buck," "taking the bull by the horns," and "going for the whole ball of wax"? Unfortunately, these phrases *never* die! A young person hears for the first time that something "is the greatest thing since sliced bread," is amused, sticks it in his memory bank, and unwittingly extends its shelf life by recirculating it. We suspect that eliminating clichés is more difficult than changing a fan belt with the engine running. So let's belly-up and try harder!

COUNTERPOINT

Note on office bulletin board.

> This department requires no physical fitness program. Everyone gets enough exercise jumping to conclusions, flying off the handle, carrying things too far, dodging responsibilities, and pushing his luck.

Get Started Now

POINT

The brain is a true marvel; it functions reliably from birth and only stops when we stand before an audience. This stand-and-speak phenomenon is similar to the sit-and-write shutdown. One solution to the brain drain is to sit and immediately record *anything* that comes to mind, thereby setting the pattern for writing whatever was intended. Better yet, if we record bits and pieces of data *when first contemplated,* our notes will provide the initial momentum. Many report success in visualizing both the end product and themselves actually writing it. Now if you're lucky, what you "see" is what you'll get.

COUNTERPOINT

Writing a first paragraph is like raising a first child. It's better if you start out on the second.

—Lynn Z. Bloom
Researcher on "anxious writing"

Atone Rather Than Bemoan

POINT

Possibly the two most difficult words to write are "I'm sorry"—especially when followed by "I don't know," "I don't understand," or "I'm wrong." If these expressions were not so pain inducing, we'd rely less upon various word ploys such as avoidance ("It wasn't *my* responsibility") or defensiveness ("A decision had to be made and I made it!"). Let's admit that "circumlocutory evasion" never clarified anything. And while the situation seems hopeless, it probably isn't serious. The shortest distance between two points of view is often a straight line of apology.

COUNTERPOINT

To apologize is to lay the foundation for a future offense.

—Ambrose Bierce

Forgive the Sender

POINT

While writing is a serious activity, it needn't be a solemn one. All office workers collect memorable memos. A claims adjuster receives this classic from a policyholder: "If the other driver had stopped a few yards behind himself, it certainly wouldn't have happened." Or a human services intake counselor reports this gem: "Mrs. Smith hasn't had any clothes for a year and had been visited by the clergy regularly." Shared in staff meetings, stapled on bulletin boards, and savored eternally, these messages are precious. But between the laughs, we can't overlook the obvious. The writers *did* communicate. We know what they meant.

COUNTERPOINT

I can't hear what you're saying because of the noise of the celery I'm chewing in my ears.

Imagine What It Would Be Like If . . .

POINT

In work settings we write objectively and appropriately. We document an employee for "intoxication," "inebriation," or "alcohol dependency." We don't describe the employee as being "gassed," "stewed," "zonked," "sloshed," or "plastered." While we normally think and speak expressively, we're restricted in "official" writings. A police report sluggishly states: "The alleged suspect was apparently apprehended while. . . ." Or a political pundit pens, "An unidentified, informed source revealed that. . . ." Although we understand why this is so, wouldn't it be refreshing to read, just once, that "the crook was collared" or that "Senator whomever squealed"?

COUNTERPOINT

We are weak, not because our vocabulary is inadequate, but because we are stale in the way we use it.

—HUGH WALPOLE

Now Hear This!

POINT

All is not lost. Occasionally, a champion for clarity emerges. Navy Secretary John Lehman deserves the "Return to the Real Thing" award. He restored venerable naval expressions by edict. "Enlisted personnel housing" is once again, officially, "the barracks." Likewise, "floor" is "deck," "upstairs" is "topside," and "stairs" are "ladders." Thus Secretary Lehman provides a service for his service. And grasp the *power* of writing something like, "Henceforth, all 'walls' will be designated by their rightful, historical designation—'bulkheads.'" Wow!

COUNTERPOINT

The Way It Had Become	The Way It Really Was Once And Forever Will Be
enlisted dining facility	mess deck
unaccompanied officer personnel housing	bachelor officer's quarters
Navy correctional facility	brig

Carefully Exercise Your Expertise

POINT

Writers can easily deceive by exploiting a reader's perception of the writer's credibility. According to the "Dr. Fox" hypothesis: "An unintelligible communication from a legitimate source in the recipient's area of expertise will increase the recipient's rating of the author's competence." Lawrence J. Peter's early warning that "an ounce of image is worth a pound of performance" still prevails. Or as marketing professor J. Scott Armstrong notes, "If you can't convince them, confuse them."

COUNTERPOINT

Only intuition can protect you from the most dangerous individual of all—the articulate incompetent.

—ROBERT BERNSTEIN, Publisher

Keep in Touch

POINT

Because all human relationships are perpetually tentative, the very important ones deserve frequent reinforcement. Obviously, face-to-face communication has the greatest potential for bonding relationships. And the telephone, indeed, helps us to "reach out and touch someone." Written messages, however, provide another benefit—a lasting and tangible verbal link that, until revoked, is irrevocable. Perhaps that's why "deeds of trust" are always written.

COUNTERPOINT

You have to keep people informed even if you're lying.

—RON MCDOLE
Ex-Washington Redskin

Cite the Source

POINT

While speech is free, writing can be costly if not original. Any written material protected by copyright can't be "borrowed" with impunity. As Wilson Mizner noted, "If you steal from one author it's plagiarism; if you steal from many, it's research." Whenever we use someone's thoughts, ideas, or materials—even if they are without copyright—it's simply good form and practice to cite the source. Not only do we protect ourselves, but we also add credibility to our own writing by bolstering it with the voices and words of authority.

COUNTERPOINT

Your manuscript is both good and original; but the part that is good is not original, and the part that is original is not good.

—SAMUEL JOHNSON

Punctuate for Clarity

POINT

Punctuation is a bugaboo for most. Some "rules" like "omit the comma before 'as,' 'for,' and 'since' in a sentence-ending adverbial clause," are hard to recall—as if anyone cares! And what a mess that sentence is. Despite commas, quotes, quotes-within-quotes, dashes, hyphens, and exclamation points, at least we didn't violate *that* "rule." Perhaps only a language purist objects when such violations occur. The *one* rule to remember: If a punctuation mark is needed for clarity, use it!

COUNTERPOINT

Jim thought Sam really blew the account.
Jim, thought Sam, really blew the account.
Question: Who "blew the account"?

Quantify When It Counts

POINT

Phrases connoting numbers are imprecise. How many of whatever, for example, are "a few" or "several"? Don Ried has provided "absolute values for common American phrases denoting nonspecific quantities." Therefore, according to Ried: 2–4 are "a couple"; 3–5 are "a few"; 3–6 are "quite a few"; 3–8 are "many"; and 3–9 are "several." The message is clear. Precise numbers are required when we want to be understood accurately. But when such accuracy is unnecessary, we can leave our reader free to interpret our numerical phrases with vast differences in meaning. Naturally, there is a "whole bunch" of meanings for "vast."

COUNTERPOINT

Absolute Values for Interpreting Survey Results

A majority	50% + 1
A clear majority	50%
A vast majority	52% to 60%
An overwhelming majority	61% to 70%
Almost everyone	71% to 75%
Practically everyone	76% to 80%
Everyone	81% to 85%
Absolutely everyone	86% to 90%
100% of those surveyed	91% to 95%

—Don Ried

Put Probing Questions in Writing

POINT

Our writing informs, influences, interprets, inspires, and occasionally incites. We also inquire. While penetrating questions in conversation can be unnerving or embarrassing, written probes allow time for thoughtful response. The carefully phrased written question often elicits insights that would be undiscovered or lost in normal conversation. As Gertrude Stein noted, "Suppose no one asked a question. What would the answer be?"

COUNTERPOINT

The uncreative mind can spot wrong answers, but it takes a creative mind to spot wrong questions.

—ANTONY JAY

Write to Yourself

POINT

Since most of us shun writing anything except under some duress, it may be risky to suggest writing as a vehicle for understanding ourselves. Psychologist Jean Piaget noted, "I wrote even if only for myself. I could not think unless I did so." While introspective writing allows us to keep in touch with ourselves, reading what we write enables us to review and refine our thinking. These recorded occasional insights and distracting scraps can be drawn upon later when we're writing for a wider audience.

COUNTERPOINT

I write entirely to find out what I'm thinking, what I'm looking at, what I see and what it means. What I want and what I fear.

—JOAN DIDION

Enhance the Image

POINT

How the message looks can be as important as what it says. The most carefully worded letter is weakened by skewed spacing or mangled margins. The letter-perfect missive from a word processor evokes a negative image when dispatched on a crummy letterhead. Even an informal, handwritten note to a colleague lacks credibility when penned under "From the Desk of Whatsizname." While perfection in the printing can't overcome imperfections in the writing, faulty printing does evoke second thoughts about the sender.

COUNTERPOINT

Writing must be dramatic, brief, strikingly phrased, memorable, novel, and able to withstand repetition.

—Author Unknown

—and enhance the writer's image.

Consider Artificial Intelligence

POINT

Can't remember the rules? Grammar books don't help? Your colleagues know even less? Computer software to the rescue! Impressive artificial intelligence packages can correct errors or suggest optional phrasing. Goodbye to misspellings, redundancies, clichés, split infinitives, and dangling participles! Our only remaining dilemma is *what* to write. Despair not. Enter books containing model letters for any and all exigencies. And somewhere, we suspect, there's yet another software package to make this final selection for us.

COUNTERPOINT

So Much for Artificial Intelligence

News Item: A computer, programmed to translate English into Russian, was fed the phrase: "Out of sight, out of mind." A reversing of the process yielded, "Invisible insanity."

Use One-Pulse Words

POINT

If we drop the long words and just use short ones that are known by most of us, why not take it one more step and write with one-pulse words? We cite Jim Grant as the sire and Dave Blum as the vox of the one-pulse way to write with wit and vim sans words of two beats or more. Now that you have read all of these one-pulse words, you know that while they may be clear, they can soon drive one right out of his or her skull.

ONE MORE POINT

The One-Pulse Pledge to the Flag

> I pledge my troth to the flag of the states that are joined in this land and to the form of rule for which it stands; one large state with trust in God, not to be split, in which all can be free and for whom the law is just.

—ANNE DAVIS TOPPINS

Cite the Bullet

POINT

Another aid to readability is the use of dot points or bullets. They can be inserted to replace 1-2-3 listings whenever serial order is irrelevant. Bullets are most effective when started with an action verb and followed by a minimum of words. Key ideas thus can be highlighted and located amid a morass of text. So write it tight and cite the bullet.

COUNTERPOINT

BULLETS

- Facilitate reading
- Reduce verbiage
- Focus attention
- Emphasize ideas
- Reinforce points

Sign Off Clearly

POINT

How do you respond to someone who signs off as "P. J. Smith" or "Pat Smith"? Do you write "Dear Mr.," "Dear Mrs.," "Dear Miss," or "Dear Ms"? Of course the less formal "Dear P. J." or "Dear Pat" is acceptable. Fortunately, conventions change. Recall the dilemma when answering "Patty" before the interchangeable "Ms" became popular? Does a letter writer deliberately confuse his or her reader? If you are "Pat," please consider signing off as "Patricia" or "Patrick," or whatever until we know you personally.

COUNTERPOINT

A deserving response to the "sexless" writer: Dear Sir and/or Madam:

Exude Appropriate Warmth

POINT

If you're so inclined *and really mean it,* add a touch of cordiality to your letters. But be forewarned: bogus blessings and phony platitudes can obviously erode an otherwise effective message.

What I Write:	*What my reader might think:*
I'll try to contact you prior to our next meeting.	"*Try*" to contact me? What does he mean by "prior"?
I look forward to working with you.	Does he *really* "enjoy" working with me?
Let's plan to have lunch together next Thursday just prior to our meeting. I'm looking forward to working with you on this assignment.	He *wants* to see me for lunch on Thursday. I'll arrange it. Working with him is a pleasure.

COUNTERPOINT

It takes two of us to create truth; one to utter it and one to understand it.

—Kahlil Gibran

Wait—In Time You Might Be Dead Right

POINT

Perhaps we shouldn't be disrespectful toward the professional grammarians. After all, it is they who alert us to our penned sins. But they're all so picky, and a few are stuffy besides. And *violent!* Who else is so bewitched by *split* infinitives, *dangled* modifiers, and *neutered* pronouns? Is that what they mean when they accuse the rest of us of *"killing* the King's English"? Fortunately, the last hurrah is ours. Sooner or later our mistakes prevail in perpetuity. Well, for a long time, anyway.

COUNTERPOINT

Language rests upon use; anything used long enough by enough people will become standard.

—CHARLTON LAIRD

Exorcize the IZE's

POINT

We can improve our business communications imme-diately by simply *not* adding "-ized" (strategized), "-ment" (time-phasement), "-wise" (suggestionwise), or "-tion" (utilization) to words. Regrettably, but appropriately, it's called "nominalizing." You ask, "What's wrong with utiliza-tion?" Invariably, whenever you read this word, the writer could more accurately and simply have used "use." Now, won't you help finalize this practice by circularizing it among your colleagues?

COUNTERPOINT

Practice will smartenize your style.

—JOSEPH C. PATTISON
"How to Write an F Paper"

Dictate to Yourself

POINT

Once ready to write, many find that the rapid flow of their ideas is drained away by their slow writing speed. Direct dictation, normally a perk associated with status, frees one entirely from the act of writing. And those who have mastered keyboard entry skills can approach the speed of thought. If, however, you have neither status nor skill, there are options. Hastily list key words only and then backtrack by writing out the missing material. Or dictate to yourself on cassette tape. Then, replay and write.

COUNTERPOINT

Have you ever wondered what an *exact* transcript of a boss's letter to a secretary might reveal?

Today's date
To John—Hey, George, how does
John spell his last name? S-m-y-t-h-e?
John Smythe
Look his address up

Dear John:

I am writing to give you the final estimate on the piping for the project.

Harry—how much was the Smythe estimate? 3 thou? OK, we'll make it 32 hundred for the idiot way he spells his name.

We have enjoyed the chance to work with you on this project, blah, blah, blah,

Close it and
Sign it.
—Pryor Report

95

The Report—Define the Problem

POINT

Most middle managers in the business sector and other professionals at all levels write reports with varying frequency. The next few pages highlight various phases of a report-writing cycle. The first phase, defining the problem, is often the most difficult. The supreme challenge, of course, is to complete this sentence *in twenty-five words or less:* The purpose of this report is to.... And this sentence should be written *before* a single word of the actual report is recorded!

COUNTERPOINT

The *perfect* problem statement is:

- Brief,
- Clear,
- Precise,
- Accurate,
- Relevant,
- Complete,
- Defensible, and ...
- Workable!

The Report—Develop a Work Plan

POINT

To assure staying on schedule and to avoid straying off target, devise a simple time-task schedule. By listing the tasks to be accomplished on the vertical axis and by indicating the estimated time requirements along the horizontal, we can monitor the writing process.

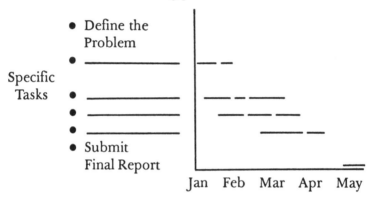

TIME LINE

We are also beginning to envision the final product in terms of scope, depth, length, and format.

COUNTERPOINT

It is never prudent to make vast plans with half-vast ideas.

The Report—Gather Relevant Data

POINT

Sources of report data include direct observations, various records, test results, and interviews. For the interview formulate a set of key questions and, if possible, refine them in rehearsal. This interview "guide" virtually assures us of getting only the data we want and, equally important, of not getting the data we don't want. Why overload the circuits? The actual writing process begins as we accurately record and systematically cluster all relevant findings.

COUNTERPOINT

A little inaccuracy saves a world of explanation.

—C. E. AYRES

The Report—Process Findings

POINT

Obviously, accurate and complete findings form the basis for any report. Without them there is no report. And if they are handled improperly there is no credibility. Veteran report writers analyze, synthesize, and synergize findings while simultaneously drawing *tentative* conclusions from them. This practice differs markedly from the "Don't-confuse-me-with-the-facts,-my-mind's-already-made-up" approach. The making of tentative judgments enables the expansion of hunches, elicits a verification of collected findings, and encourages a search for additional corroboration.

COUNTERPOINT

A way of seeing is also a way of not seeing—a focus upon Object A involves a neglect of Object B.

—JOHN DEWEY

The Report—Develop Conclusions

POINT

We derive conclusions directly and exclusively from findings. Any written conclusions not logically linked to specific findings are invalid. Once a reader detects the slightest break in this necessary link, the writer's credibility is shattered. Only when conclusions naturally grow and flow from documentable findings can the reader trust the writer. And, after all, that's what it's about.

COUNTERPOINT

A scientific paper . . . a cunningly contrived piece of rhetoric . . . has only one purpose; it must persuade the reader of the veracity of the observer, his disinterestedness, his logical infallibility, and the complete necessity of his conclusions.

—J. M. ZIMAN

The Report—Generate Recommendations

POINT

After reporting findings and conclusions, we prepare the final phase of the logical chain—recommendations. Just as conclusions are drawn from findings, so are recommendations the natural yield of conclusions. Normally, we arrange recommendations by priority and sequence, fine-tune them consistent with the problem statement, provide options whenever appropriate, and commit them to print in a manner most likely to secure their acceptance.

COUNTERPOINT

The recommendations are free. It won't cost anything until you start to follow them.

WRITE IT RIGHT NO. 82

The Report—Prepare for Print

POINT

Once the final draft survives the last accuracy and editing checks, it is ready for printing and distribution. How the report looks—cover, color, graphics, type style, paper grade—can enhance its impact. The old analogy of "the-right-clothes-don't-open-doors-but-the-wrong-ones-can-close-them" prevails. While a lousy report can't be improved by good reproduction, an outstanding report can be diminished by inept reproduction. And remember— good reports become building blocks; lousy ones, bookends.

COUNTERPOINT

To gain maximum attention, it's difficult to beat a good, big, and expensive mistake.

The Report—Attach a Summary

POINT

One dictum applies to all report writers: No report should ever be longer than it has to be. Some corporations have a second, practical dictum: Regardless of length, all reports must be accompanied by a one-page summary or abstract. This brief overview (1) indicates if the entire report is required reading, (2) allows very busy people to be reasonably familiar with the material prior to a careful study, (3) provides a handy document for later review, and (4) permits a quick, easy, and inexpensive transmittal of key points.

COUNTERPOINT

If you can't summarize your recommendations on a single page, you haven't solved the problem yet.

WRITE IT RIGHT NO. 84
Allow for Editing Time

POINT

Editing isn't easy. It isn't a quick fix, either. Often, editing a single-page memo, directive, or letter consumes more time than the actual writing. More care is needed to ensure that the message received by our reader is as similar as possible to the one we intend to send. In conversation we have the luxury of instant correction. In writing we don't. It takes time to be right the first time.

COUNTERPOINT

Interviewer:	"How long does it take you to prepare a ten-minute speech?"
Woodrow Wilson:	"Two weeks."
Interviewer:	"How long for an hour speech?"
Woodrow Wilson:	"One week."
Interviewer:	"How long for a two-hour speech?"
Woodrow Wilson:	"I'm ready now!"

Quash the Qualifiers

POINT

Were you once urged to sow adjectives and adverbs amid your prose? A memo from your boss cites the "exceedingly fine" job you did in compiling a report. Your last effort elicited an "outstanding." What aspect of your report deserved commendation? You don't know. And was the "outstanding" report better or worse than the "exceedingly fine" one? Qualifiers like "good," "a lot of," and "a great deal" lack specificity. "Good" is better than what? How many are "a lot of"? How much is "a great deal"? Too much, probably.

COUNTERPOINT

He: "Have a good day!"
She: "Thanks, but I have other plans."

WRITE IT RIGHT NO. 86
Respect Creativity

POINT

Most of the writing we do at work is predictably uninspiring. When a situation invites a touch of inventiveness, we can heed President Takashi Ishihara of the Nissan Motor Company: "The first step in the creative process should be to resist the temptation to imitate." We'll ignore the counter quip of Franklin P. Jones: "Originality is the art of concealing your source." Though imagination is intelligence at play, we can ill afford to conceal inspired moments at work—at least on occasion.

COUNTERPOINT

No machine, no electronic wizardry, can replace the single act of creation, the inspired moment that arrives in its own speed, and from its own unknown source. It is what drives all the rest. Regardless of how technology increases the speed, the volume, and the nature of communication, the value of the content—the very essence—will begin and end with the creative personality."

> —GILBERT GROSVENOR
> President, National Geographic Society

Protect Your Space

POINT

To write more than a short memo one needs personal space—uninterrupted, inviolate, inspirational. And quiet. Environmental noise includes telephones and unexpected visitors. Among the latter is the hovering boss. Two hours following your receipt of a week-long writing assignment the boss, lurking in your doorway, asks if you've started. And two days later this hoverer, seeking a rough draft, again pops your space bubble.

COUNTERPOINT

Employee: "I can't write anything when you stand behind me like that!"

Colleague: "Who was standing behind you on that *last* report? You couldn't have done such a lousy job all by yourself."

Write On!

POINT

A friend confides, "Bob, you write because you're good at it and you enjoy it." My flippant retort: "The only writing I enjoy is endorsing royalty checks." Writing to me is both frustrating and fatiguing. And I'm *not* particularly "good at it." A lifetime of putting ideas on paper will not yield enough deserving words, for example, to displace one paragraph in Ernest Hemingway's *The Old Man and the Sea.* Now, *that's* good writing! I remain intrigued, however, by our attempts to deliver marketplace messages with our verbal jottings. If you have found but a single useful suggestion, then my mission is accomplished. Here's to short reports, "demo" memos, and better letters!

COUNTERPOINT

Writing is easy. I just open a vein and bleed.

—RED SMITH

And, in Conclusion

POINT

It's time for us to stop, revise again, allow an editor to fine-tune, and await publication. Applying the suggestions in this volume will enhance your business-related memos, letters, and reports. If we were to underscore a few points for emphasis, they would be:

- You can improve your writing only if you want to.
- Respect the "rules" of writing but do not be intimidated by them.
- Keep your reader in mind whenever you write.
- Write no more than your reader needs to know.
- Freely express your thoughts in writing, *then* revise.
- Ask a colleague to read what you've written.
- Before distributing anything you've written, check one final time for accuracy, brevity, and clarity.

Send a note to this writer by way of the publisher. Your reactions and suggestions *are* invited.

COUNTERPOINT

. . . so there ain't nothing more to write about, and I am rotten glad of it, because if I'd a knowed what a trouble it was to make a book I wouldn't a'tackled it, and ain't a going to no more.

—MARK TWAIN
The Adventures of Huckleberry Finn